DEAR SELF

—✧ – ✧—

BLOOM BOOK

DEAR SELF

—◊ – ◊—

BLOOM BOOK

100 Prompts to Honor, Appreciate, and Deepen Your Connection with Yourself

Tammy Blalock

Published by Texas Camp Gal Press, Christine, Texas
ISBN Number: 978-1-970501-17-9

DEDICATION

For me.

The one who cherished every victory and survived every fracture. Each moment brought me here—learning presence, clarity, and the quiet discipline of the mind.

"Nothing can dim the light which shines from within."

—Maya Angelou

CONTENTS

FORWARD

I wrote this book series (Burn & Bloom) because I wanted to. Because after learning to release pain, I needed to remember what it feels like to celebrate love — the kind that heals, sustains, and inspires.

No one really prepares you for how beautiful a healthy relationship can be — how grounding it feels to be seen, valued, and understood. This book is a tribute to those connections that bring peace to our hearts and light to our days. It's about the people who remind us that love can be safe, steady, and true.

Healthy relationships don't erase our pain; they help us carry it differently. They teach us patience, grace, and the quiet strength that comes from being loved without conditions.

If you're holding this book, I imagine you've known a love worth honoring — a relationship that's brought meaning, laughter, or growth into your life. This is your space to celebrate that. To reflect on the beauty of connection and the small, sacred ways love continues to bloom.

May these pages help you give thanks for the relationships that root you, the people who water your soul, and the moments that remind you that love — in all its forms — is still the most extraordinary thing we'll ever know.

With Love,
Tammy

ACKNOWLEDGMENTS

This book series was born from both pain and purpose. I never set out to write something like this — I just needed a place to put the things I couldn't say out loud. What started as personal healing became something I now know so many others needed too.

To my daughters, Sierra and Kyanna — you are my greatest teachers and the truest reflections of my heart. I hope you are always loved with the same tenacity, stubbornness, and strength with which I love you both. May you always know your worth, chase your joy, and never doubt the power of your own light.

To my three beautiful grandchildren, Archie, Kamari, Khloe — and any future ones who find their way into this world — may you always know love that lifts you, friendships that steady you, and relationships that are cherished, healthy, and mutually beneficial.

May you never be betrayed by someone you love.

May you always be surrounded by people who see your light and protect your peace and whose loyalty is unwavering, absolute, and steadfast.

And may you grow up knowing that your worth is never measured by how others treat you, but by the kindness, strength, and honesty you carry within yourself.

And to my dearest friend, Yoli — your loyalty, support, and unwavering presence have been a constant source of comfort and strength. You have shown me what steadfast love and true sisterhood can look like, and I will always be grateful for the way you've stood beside me through every season of life.

To every person who will open this book and see themselves somewhere between the lines — I honor your courage. I know this journey isn't easy. I wrote these pages for you, for the nights that feel too heavy, for the mornings that feel like survival, and for the moment when you realize you've made it through.

And finally, to the quiet power that moves through all of us — God, Allah, Yahweh, the Divine, the Great Spirit, the Light within — thank you for teaching me that burning can also be a form of blooming.

DISCLAIMER

I am not a medical or psychological professional, and nothing in this book should be taken as medical or mental health advice. The reflections and prompts within these pages are simply meant to inspire gratitude, connection, and deeper appreciation for the relationships that enrich your life.

These pages were created with care and intention — to uplift, not instruct; to celebrate, not analyze. Use them in the spirit they were designed: as a space to honor love, express joy, and reflect on the beauty of genuine connection.

INTRODUCTION

There are moments in life when love becomes complicated — when the people we once trusted most become the ones who wound us deepest. And there are other moments, equally powerful, when we remember that healing is still possible.

This is where **Burn + Bloom** lives — in that sacred space between heartbreak and hope.

These journals were born from the belief that our stories deserve a home, even the messy ones. Inside these pages, you'll find a place to speak the words you never could, to write the letters you never sent, to name the pain you've carried quietly for far too long. You'll find prompts that help you unearth what still aches — and others that help you see what's still beautiful.

Because healing isn't about pretending it never happened. It's about facing what did and choosing to grow anyway.

The **Burn Books** are for release — a space to unravel, to scream on paper, to pour out every sharp edge of hurt you've kept hidden. They're meant to be cleansing, confronting, and ultimately freeing.

When you've finished one, you may choose to keep it — or destroy it. **Burn it. Shred it. Sink it. Let it go however you need to.** The ritual is yours. It doesn't have to be perfect — it only has to be honest. Release it when you're ready, knowing that the act itself is the exhale after holding your breath for far too long.

The **Bloom Books** are for renewal — a softer space to remember love, gratitude, and peace. They're about noticing what still lives inside you after the fire, about watering what remains, and watching it grow into something new. When you've completed your Bloom Book, you hold more than pages — you hold proof of healing. **Keep it as a memento. Gift it to someone you love. Leave it for a stranger to find. Wrap it in ribbon and tuck it away for your children or grandchildren to find one day.** Let it serve as a gentle reminder that growth is never wasted, and love — even imperfect love — always leaves something worth keeping.

You can't have one without the other. Every burn leaves room for a bloom.

I created this series not as a writer or a therapist, but as a human being who's been broken, healed, and broken again.

These pages are part confession, part conversation, and part invitation — an invitation to join me in the work of becoming whole.

So take your time here. Be honest. Be unfiltered. Be brave enough to tell yourself the truth.

This is your story. Your ashes. Your bloom.

Tammy Blalock
Founder & Creator, **Burn + Bloom**

REST STOPS

Throughout this journal, you'll find intentional Rest Stops placed after each major section. These are not fillers — they are moments of stillness and appreciation.

The *Bloom* journey invites you to slow down, reflect, and savor the goodness that surrounds you. Growth isn't only found in doing — it's also found in pausing, breathing, and simply being present with the beauty of now.

Each Rest Stop includes a mandala coloring page for mindful relaxation and a positive affirmation or quote to inspire calm and gratitude. Take your time here. Color, journal, or simply rest in quiet thought.

These pauses are gentle reminders that joy lives in the in-between moments — in reflection, in peace, and in the space you give yourself to just *be*.

Breathe. Reflect. Bloom again.

EARLY MEMORIES & CONNECTION

Date:____________________ Emotional Check-In:____________________

What early memories shaped the way I learned to love myself?

Date:____________________ Emotional Check-In:____________________

When did I first feel a sense of inner strength?

Date:____________________ Emotional Check-In:____________________

What did I admire most about myself as a child?

Date:____________________ Emotional Check-In:____________________

How did I learn to cope, adapt, or survive?

Date:____________________ Emotional Check-In:____________________

When did I first realize I was capable of more than I believed?

Date:____________________ Emotional Check-In:____________________

What parts of my childhood self still live inside me today?

Date:____________________ Emotional Check-In:____________________

How did I learn to seek comfort, safety, or belonging?

Date:____________________ Emotional Check-In:____________________

What early experiences taught me resilience?

Date:____________________ Emotional Check-In:____________________

What moments of joy or curiosity defined my younger self?

Date:____________________ Emotional Check-In:____________________

How did I begin forming a relationship with who I am?

—◇ – ◇—

"To love oneself is the beginning of a lifelong romance." — **Oscar Wilde**

Early Memories & Connection

Self-love begins in remembering who you were before the world told you who to be.

When you return to your earliest self, what truths still feel like home?

SUPPORT & UNDERSTANDING

Date:____________________ Emotional Check-In:____________________

How do I show up for myself during difficult moments?

Date:____________________ Emotional Check-In:____________________

What does emotional support look like when it comes from within?

Date:____________________ Emotional Check-In:____________________

When did I begin understanding my own needs more clearly?

Date:____________________ Emotional Check-In:____________________

How do I comfort myself when no one else is available?

Date:____________________ Emotional Check-In:____________________

What helps me feel grounded when life feels heavy?

Date:____________________ Emotional Check-In:____________________

How do I validate my own feelings without judgment?

Date:____________________ Emotional Check-In:____________________

What does inner understanding feel like in my body?

Date:____________________ Emotional Check-In:____________________

How do I honor my limits without guilt?

Date:____________________ Emotional Check-In:____________________

When have I surprised myself with my own strength?

Date:____________________ Emotional Check-In:____________________

What kind of support do I want to offer myself moving forward?

—◊ – ◊—

"You yourself, as much as anybody in the entire universe, deserve your love and affection." **— Buddha**

Support & Understanding

Understanding yourself is the doorway to healing — the moment you stop apologizing for needing care.

When you think about how far you've come, how does your own strength inspire you to keep going?

GROWTH & REFLECTION

Date:____________________ Emotional Check-In:____________________

How have I grown in the last few years?

Date:____________________ Emotional Check-In:____________________

What challenges pushed me toward becoming a better version of myself?

Date:____________________ Emotional Check-In:____________________

Which habits no longer serve who I am becoming?

Date:____________________ Emotional Check-In:____________________

How do I honor my evolution while respecting my past?

Date:____________________ Emotional Check-In:____________________

What parts of me still need nurturing or attention?

Date:____________________ Emotional Check-In:____________________

When did I last outgrow a version of myself?

Date:____________________ Emotional Check-In:____________________

How do I measure progress without comparison?

Date:____________________ Emotional Check-In:____________________

What patterns am I ready to release?

Date:____________________ Emotional Check-In:____________________

What mistakes taught me the most?

Date:____________________ Emotional Check-In:____________________

What have I learned about myself through change?

—◇ – ◇—

"And the day came when the risk to remain tight in a bud was more painful than the risk it took to blossom." — Anaïs Nin

Growth & Reflection

Growth invites you to bloom into who you were always meant to be.

When you reflect on your evolution, what new truth do you now see clearly?

SHARED JOY & CELEBRATION

Date:____________________ Emotional Check-In:____________________

What bring me joy in my everyday life?

Date:____________________ Emotional Check-In:____________________

How do I celebrate myself in small, meaningful ways?

Date:____________________ Emotional Check-In ____________________

What activities make me feel alive and present?

Date:____________________ Emotional Check-In:____________________

When do I feel the purest form of happiness?

Date:____________________ Emotional Check-In:____________________

How do I honor my own achievements?

Date:____________________ Emotional Check-In:____________________

What makes me laugh freely and fully?

Date:____________________ Emotional Check-In:____________________

What simple pleasures brighten my days?

Date:____________________ Emotional Check-In:____________________

How do I create joy even in difficult seasons?

Date:____________________ Emotional Check-In:____________________

When did I last celebrate my own growth?

Date:____________________ Emotional Check-In:____________________

What experiences make me grateful to be me?

—✧ – ✧—

"Joy is a net of love by which you can catch souls." — **Mother Teresa**

Shared Joy & Celebration

Joy grows when you give yourself permission to feel it without apology.

When you look at your happiest moments, what do they reveal about what you need more of in your life?

STRENGTH & RESILIENCE

Date:____________________ Emotional Check-In ____________________

What difficult seasons have shaped my inner strength?

Date:____________________ Emotional Check-In:____________________

How have I learned to stand back up after being knocked down?

Date:____________________ Emotional Check-In:____________________

What do I admire most about my own resilience?

Date:____________________ Emotional Check-In:____________________

When have I been stronger than anyone realized?

Date:____________________ Emotional Check-In____________________

What hardships taught me the most about myself?

Date:____________________ Emotional Check-In:____________________

How do I protect my peace during chaos?

Date:____________________ Emotional Check-In:____________________

What strengths do I often forget I have?

Date:____________________ Emotional Check-In:____________________

How do I rebuild when life forces me to start over?

Date:____________________ Emotional Check-In:____________________

What obstacles have I already survived?

Date:____________________ Emotional Check-In:____________________

How do I honor the parts of me that refuse to give up?

—✧ – ✧—

"Still, like air, I'll rise." — **Maya Angelou**

Strength & Resilience

Your resilience is the quiet power that has carried you this far — and will carry you further still.

When you consider everything you've overcome, what does that say about who you truly are?

ADMIRATION & APPRECIATION

Date:____________________ Emotional Check-In:____________________

What do I genuinely admire about myself?

Date:____________________ Emotional Check-In:____________________

Which of my traits make me proud?

Date:____________________ Emotional Check-In:____________________

What talents, abilities, or gifts do I too often overlook?

Date:____________________ Emotional Check-In:____________________

How do I show myself appreciation?

Date:____________________ Emotional Check-In:____________________

What am I grateful to myself for surviving?

Date:____________________ Emotional Check-In:____________________

What accomplishments deserve to be recognized?

Date:____________________ Emotional Check-In:____________________

Which parts of myself deserve more kindness?

Date:____________________ Emotional Check-In:____________________

How do I celebrate my own uniqueness?

Date:____________________ Emotional Check-In:____________________

What makes me someone worth loving?

Date:____________________ Emotional Check-In:____________________

What do I hope I never stop appreciating about myself?

—◇ – ◇—

"To love oneself is to understand that we are a work in progress and a masterpiece at the same time." — Unknown

Admiration & Appreciation

Appreciation grows when you finally see yourself through eyes of compassion, not critique.

When you speak kindly to yourself, what shifts inside you?

LESSONS & LEGACY

Date:____________________ Emotional Check-In:____________________

What life lessons have shaped who I am today?

Date:____________________ Emotional Check-In:____________________

What values guide the way I live?

Date:____________________ Emotional Check-In:____________________

What wisdom have I gained from pain or loss?

Date:____________________ Emotional Check-In:____________________

How do I want to be remembered by the people I love?

Date:____________________ Emotional Check-In:____________________

What parts of my story feel the most important?

Date:____________________ Emotional Check-In:____________________

What teachings do I want to pass forward?

Date:____________________ Emotional Check-In:____________________

What has time revealed about my priorities?

Date:____________________ Emotional Check-In:____________________

What truths have stayed with me through every chapter?

Date:____________________ Emotional Check-In:____________________

Which experiences defined the person I became?

Date:____________________ Emotional Check-In:____________________

What legacy do I hope to leave behind, even in small ways?

⟡ – ⟡

"The meaning of life is to find your gift. The purpose of life is to give it away."
— Pablo Picasso

Lessons & Legacy

Your legacy is written quietly — in your choices, your growth, and your courage to keep becoming.

When you think about the story you're writing, what do you want it to say about you?

CONNECTION & COMMUNICATION

Date:____________________ Emotional Check-In:____________________

How do I communicate with myself when I'm hurting?

Date:____________________ Emotional Check-In:____________________

What internal dialogue do I want to change?

Date:____________________ Emotional Check-In:____________________

How do I reconnect when I feel disconnected from myself?

Date:____________________ Emotional Check-In:____________________

What helps me return to center?

Date:____________________ Emotional Check-In:____________________

How do I listen to my intuition more closely?

Date:____________________ Emotional Check-In:____________________

What truths am I avoiding that need my attention?

Date:____________________ Emotional Check-In:____________________

How can I speak to myself with more honesty and compassion?

Date:____________________ Emotional Check-In:____________________

When do I feel most aligned with who I truly am?

Date:____________________ Emotional Check-In:____________________

What practices strengthen my connection to myself?

Date:____________________ Emotional Check-In:____________________

How do I rebuild trust within myself after breaking it?

—⟡ – ⟡—

"The quieter you become, the more you are able to hear." — Rumi

Connection & Communication

Self-connection grows in silence — where truth has room to speak.
When you listen inward, what truth rises first?

—◊ – ◊—

GRATITUDE & PRESENCE

Date:____________________ Emotional Check-In:____________________

What am I most grateful for about myself today?

Date:____________________ Emotional Check-In:____________________

How does gratitude shift the way I see my life?

Date:____________________ Emotional Check-In:____________________

What brings peace into my daily routine?

Date:____________________ Emotional Check-In:____________________

How do I stay grounded when I feel overwhelmed?

Date:____________________ Emotional Check-In:____________________

What moments make me feel truly present?

Date:____________________ Emotional Check-In:____________________

How has practicing gratitude changed me?

Date:____________________ Emotional Check-In:____________________

What do I appreciate most about the life I'm building?

Date:____________________ Emotional Check-In:____________________

How has presence helped me heal?

Date:____________________ Emotional Check-In:____________________

When do I feel closest to myself?

Date:____________________ Emotional Check-In:____________________

What gratitude practices bring me back to center?

——✧ – ✧——

***"Happiness is not something ready made. It comes from your own actions."* —**
Dalai Lama

Gratitude & Presence

Presence turns ordinary moments into anchors — reminders that your life is happening now.

When you pause in gratitude, what becomes clearer?

REFLECTION & LEGACY

Date:____________________ Emotional Check-In:____________________

What does self-love mean to me now?

Date:____________________ Emotional Check-In:____________________

How do I want to continue growing?

Date:____________________ Emotional Check-In:____________________

What parts of myself need more care or softness?

Date:____________________ Emotional Check-In:____________________

How do I honor the woman I'm becoming?

Date:____________________ Emotional Check-In:____________________

What promises do I want to make to myself moving forward?

Date:____________________ Emotional Check-In:____________________

How has understanding myself changed the way I live?

Date:____________________ Emotional Check-In:____________________

What truth do I trust about who I am today?

Date:____________________ Emotional Check-In:____________________

How do I protect my peace more intentionally?

Date:____________________ Emotional Check-In:____________________

What do I want future versions of me to know?

Date:____________________ Emotional Check-In:____________________

What chapter am I ready to walk into next?

—◇ – ◇—

"Real self-love exists." — **Tammy Blalock, Founder & Creator, Burn + Bloom**

Reflection & Legacy

True self-love is reclaimed slowly — through awareness, forgiveness, and the courage to bloom again and again.

When you think about the life you're creating, what truth do you want it to rest on?

LETTER TO MY FUTURE SELF

Take a quiet moment and write a letter to your future self — the version of you who has continued to grow, love, and bloom beyond this moment.

Remind yourself of what matters most. Speak to your strength, your softness, your gratitude, and your hope. Write about what you want to remember from this season of life — the relationships that nourish you, the lessons that grounded you, and the beauty that has unfolded around you.

Seal your letter somewhere safe — inside this book, a drawer, or an envelope you'll open one year from now. Let it serve as a reminder that growth never stops and that love — especially self-love — continues to expand with time.

Dear Me,

LEGACY

This journal is your personal garden of reflection — a living record of love, appreciation, and gratitude. When you complete it, take a moment to decide how you'd like its story to continue.

You may choose to:

- Keep it as a reminder of your journey and growth.
- Gift it to the book's subject, or to someone whose love has shaped your life.
- Pass it down to the next generation as a symbol of what it means to love, forgive, and flourish.

Whatever you decide, let it be intentional. Let it be joyful. Let it carry forward the spirit of everything you've written here — love, peace, and gratitude that continues to bloom beyond these pages.

—◊ – ◊—

Dear Reader,

____

____

____

____

____

____

____

____

____

____

MOOD TRACKER

Year:______________

	J	F	M	A	M	J	J	A	S	O	N	D
1												
2												
3												
4												
5												
6												
7												
8												
9												
10												
11												
12												
13												
14												
15												
16												
17												
18												
19												
20												
21												
22												
23												
24												
25												
26												
27												
28												
29												
30												
31												

Keys

☐ Happy
☐ Good
☐ Productive
☐ Average
☐ Sad
☐ Nervous
☐ Exhausted
☐ Bored
☐ Angry
☐ Sick

Notes

AFFIRMATIONS

I am open to giving and receiving love freely and without fear.

I am surrounded by relationships that nurture my growth and peace.

I am grateful for the people who bring light into my life.

I am worthy of healthy, balanced, and joyful connections.

I am at peace with the past and fully present in the love that remains.

I am blooming into the best version of myself through compassion and grace.

I am a reflection of the love I choose to cultivate every day.

I am ____

I am ____

I am ____

I am ____

I am ____

I am ____

I am ____

I am ____

I am ____

CRISIS & SUPPORT RESOURCES

If you or someone you love ever finds yourself in emotional distress, help is available.

If there is immediate danger, please call 911.

United States Hotlines:

- Suicide & Crisis Lifeline (988): Call or text 988 for immediate support.
- Poison Control: 1-800-222-1222
- National Domestic Violence Hotline: 1-800-799-7233 (SAFE)
- National Sexual Assault Hotline (RAINN): 1-800-656-4673
- Childhelp National Child Abuse Hotline: 1-800-422-4453
- SAMHSA Helpline (Substance Abuse & Mental Health): 1-800-662-4357
- Veterans Crisis Line: Call 988 then press 1, or text 838255

Text-Based Options:

- Crisis Text Line: Text "HELLO" to 741741 to connect.
- National Domestic Violence Hotline: Text "START" to 88788.
- Veterans Crisis Line: Text message to 838255 for help.

Other helpful numbers:

____

____

____

____

____

____

____

____

____

CLOSING

You've reached the final pages, but this isn't an ending — it's a continuation. Every word you've written here is a seed planted in gratitude, understanding, and love.

Take a moment to breathe and honor the work you've done — not just the writing, but the noticing, the remembering, the softening. You've given shape to something beautiful: the act of honoring what is good and whole within you and within the connections that have shaped your life.

Love doesn't stay still. It expands, deepens, and transforms — just like you. As you close this book, carry that love forward into your days: in the words you speak, the patience you offer, and the grace you give yourself and others.

May you continue to bloom — gently, endlessly, and always toward the light.

With Love and Understanding,
Tammy

ABOUT THE AUTHOR

Tammy Blalock is an internationally awarded live event and portrait photographer, writer, podcast host, and creator of the *Burn + Bloom* reflective journal series. A native of Atascosa County, Tammy was born in 1969 to a small Texas family defined by both fierce love and unimaginable loss. Her life has been an unfiltered mix of tenderness and tragedy — a childhood of laughter and backyard adventures shadowed by deep heartbreak and family fractures.

Tammy's story has been one of extraordinary resilience. At just fourteen, Tammy lost her youngest sister, Tanya, who was struck and killed by a speeding vehicle in 1984. Six years later, Tammy's mother died under circumstances that still ache in her memory — a loss that arrived just days after the anniversary of her sister's death. These early experiences, layered with years of complicated family dynamics, left Tammy to navigate grief, guilt, and confusion long before she had the words for them. Through every experience, she has found a way to transform suffering into purpose and vulnerability into art.

Her relationship with her last living sister became both the fire and the forge of her personal evolution. Their bond — alternating between love, rivalry, silence, and fury — ultimately became the emotional seed from which *Burn + Bloom* was born.

Tammy spent decades learning to understand the nature of trauma, forgiveness, and the delicate art of letting go. She found her voice first through photography — as an internationally awarded photojournalist who built a career capturing truth, intimacy, and fleeting emotion. Over time, that same instinct to preserve human honesty on camera evolved into a desire to help others process their own stories through words.

What began as a private healing exercise — writing through her own pain — became a mission: to help others do the same.

Deeply proud of her heritage, Tammy's family was honored in 2024 by Texas Agriculture Commissioner and inducted into the Texas Family Land Heritage Program, recognizing over 100 years of continuous agricultural ownership on the same land. The Blalock family's century-old roots in Atascosa County serve as a living reminder of perseverance, stewardship, and the importance of legacy— values that echo through each of Tammy's stories.

She continues to live and create in South Texas, where her family still tends the same land her great-grandfather once did. She spends as much time as possible with her daughters and grandchildren—her greatest joys in life—and with her father, learning the ways of ranching, the rhythm of the land, and the stories rooted in generations before her. When she's not writing or photographing, you can find her hiking, cycling, backpacking, listening to Elvis or Prince, or hunting for arrowheads across the same soil her family has cherished for more than a century.

Made in the USA
Coppell, TX
20 January 2026

68760046R00096